FOOD AND DRINK

CONTAINERS
AND THEIR PRICES

AL BERGEVIN

Cover design: Anthony Jacobson
Interior layout: Anthony Jacobson
Editor: Robert Bixby

Library of Congress Catalog
Card Number 87-51423

ISBN 0-87069-511-8

10 9 8 7 6 5 4 3 2 1

Published by

A Capital Cities/ABC, Inc. Company

Wallace-Homestead Book Company
Post Office Box 5406
Greensboro, NC 27403
(919) 275-9809

I would like to dedicate this book to my family. Their support and encouragement are deeply appreciated. My wife, Marlene, who puts up with my ranting and raving when things don't go right. My daughter, Cindy, and her husband, Steve; my son, A. J., and his wife, Deanne. To all of you a special thank you.

Contents

Foreword

With more than 1000 photographs and prices, *Food and Drink Containers and Their Prices* is a find for any collector. On each page, you'll discover valuable information, including current prices and excellent examples of food and beverage containers. It's a book for the imaginative spirit in us all.

Every page of this collection is a testimony to the value of nostalgia. The brilliant artwork represented is beautiful in its own right, but the rarity of many of the items presented has catapulted them into the realm of valued antiques. You'll find spice boxes reminiscent of voyages around the Cape of Good Hope, candy boxes your grandparents might have awakened to discover on Easter morning, syrup cans shaped like cabins in frontier villages. Here, too, are the oatmeal boxes your mother or father might have used as coin banks and drums when they were children, and cof-

fee and tea containers that conjure visions of Arabia and the Orient.

In *Food and Drink Containers and Their Prices*, Al Bergevin presents a panorama of the grocery store shelves of yesteryear, and more. Collectors everywhere have eagerly awaited this work, with its attention to detail and its up-to-date prices. They won't be disappointed.

Guide to Grading

Scale of 5 to 1

5 Mint: Brand new condition
4 Near Mint: Only slight signs of use
3 Excellent: Minor blemish, no rust
2 Good: Minor scratching and fading, minor stains
1 Fair: Scratches, some fading, some rust spots, minor dents

All prices in this book are based on near-mint condition, regardless of the condition of the example pictured.

Acknowledgments

Bill Rupp
Cedar Rapids, Iowa

Millie Vacarella
St. Paul, Minnesota

Dale Larson
St. Paul, Minnesota

A. J. and Deanne Bergevin
Mesa, Arizona

Steve Stumpf
Shoreview, Minnesota

And a very special thank you to those who wish not to be mentioned. Without your assistance, this book would not have been possible.

Introduction

More and more, one sees restaurants, specialty shops, offices, and homes decorated with antique advertising. Demand from collectors, designers, and decorators results in continued dramatic growth in antique advertising collecting.

Cleaning and restoring. The most important factor to consider when investing in a container is its condition. Condition is followed in importance by rarity and age. The buyer should examine the container for its condition before the purchase.

From the standpoint of an antiques dealer, containers should be cleaned—but not touched up—before they are sold. You, as a collector, may wish to have a container touched up for your own collection, but don't attempt to touch up a container yourself. Leave the work to an expert in restoration.

The pitfalls in cleaning and restoration may be completely unexpected. For instance, lacquer should never be used on a lithographed item because it will discolor and eventually crack and peel. When cleaning a container, never use hot or even warm water, because this will probably destroy the color. I have achieved the best and safest results with cool water, a soft rag, and a mild bar soap such as Ivory. For paper-label items, use an artist's eraser bag, which can be found at any art supply store.

Price guide and collecting. The prices in this book are based on current asking prices for containers in near mint condition. Prices may vary in different areas of the country and from dealer to dealer. It is important to remember that this is a price *guide,* not a price list.

Dimensions are in inches and are very close but are not absolutely accurate. Dimensions are listed as height, width, and depth. For example, 7 × 6 × 4 would be seven inches high, six inches wide, and four inches deep.

The serious collector would be wise to join TCCA (Tin Container Collectors Association), 11650 Riverside Drive, North Hollywood, California 91602. This organization is made up of people from all walks of life who love collecting food and beverage containers. Write to TCCA for an application form or pick one up from any member at an antiques or advertising show.

Because of the enormous variety of containers represented here, this book represents a broad overview of food and drink containers. I hope it helps you in your collecting. Antique advertising containers are among America's beautiful art forms.

Baking Powder

Calumet Bank, round, paper label,
3½ × 2, **$125**

A & P, round, lithograph, 5½ × 3, **$15**

Blue Ribbon, round, paper label, 4 × 2½, **$30**

Bakers, round, lithograph, 4½ × 3½, **$25**

Blue Ribbon, round, paper label, 5 × 3¼, **$15**

Champlain, round, paper label,
5½ × 3, **$15**

Bob-White, round, paper label,
4½ × 2½, **$15**

Musgo, round, paper label,
4½ × 2½, **$15**

C-W-S, round, paper label, 3½ × 2,
$30

Kay-W-Kay, round, paper label,
5½ × 3, **$15**

Mooney's Best, round, paper label,
5½ × 3, **$25**

Old Kentuck, pail, paper label,
4½ × 3½, **$25**

Parrot and Monkey, round, paper
label, 4 × 2½, **$40**

Our Best, round, paper label,
5½ × 3, **$15**

Pioneer, round, paper label,
5¼ × 3, **$35**

Portage, round, paper label,
5 × 3¼, **$30**

Red & White, round, lithograph,
5 × 3, **$20**

Schotten's, square, lithograph,
10 × 7 × 7, **$75**

Regal, square, lithograph,
7½ × 5½ × 5½, **$25**

Rumford, round, lithograph,
4½ × 3, **$12**

Ryzon, rectangular, paper label,
4½ × 2½ × 1½, **$10**

Snow King, round, paper label, 4½ × 3, **$20**

Washington, round, paper label, 5½ × 3, **$35**

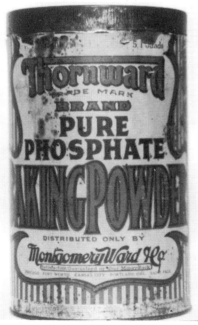

Thornward, round, paper label, 5½ × 3½, **$25**

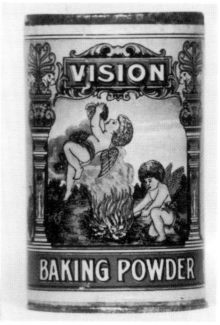

Vision, round, paper label, 4 × 2½, **$25**

Wabash, round, paper label,
3¼ × 2, **$20**

Cocoa

Baker's, square, paper label,
5 × 2½ × 2½, **$25**

Baker's, square, lithograph,
5½ × 3¼ × 3¼, **$75**

Baby Stuart, rectangular, lithograph, 6¼ × 3¼ × 2¼, **$45**

Baker's, W. G.; square; lithograph;
5 × 2½ × 2½; **$50**

Bunte, square, lithograph,
5 × 2½ × 2½, **$35**

Barker, J. H.; square; lithograph;
5 × 2½ × 2½; **$50**

Droste, square, lithograph,
6 × 3¼ × 3¼, **$25**

Daisee, rectangular, lithograph,
6 × 4½ × 3, **$40**

Grand Union, round, lithograph,
6 × 3½, **$20**

Droste's, square, lithograph,
5 × 2½ × 2½, **$45**

Droste's, square, lithograph,
6 × 3¼ × 3¼, **$35**

Hershey's, square, paper label,
4 × 2½ × 2½, **$20**

Hershey's, rectangular, paper label,
4 × 2 × 1½, **$25**

Huyler's, square, lithograph,
6 × 2½ × 2½, **$35**

Hooton's, square, lithograph,
5 × 2½ × 2½, **$45**

Iona, round, cardboard,
10½ × 4¼, **$20**

Leadway, rectangular, cardboard,
9½ × 5 × 3, **$30**

Index, square, lithograph,
8 × 6 × 6, **$50**

Lutona, rectangular, lithograph,
2 × 7 × 4½, **$30**

Mogul, rectangular, paper label,
4½ × 3¼ × 2, **$25**

Millar's, square, lithograph,
6 × 3 × 3, **$35**

Lakeland biscuits

Millar's cocoa

Daddy's Choice coffee

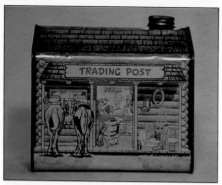

Log Cabin syrup

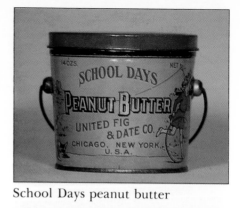

School Days peanut butter

White Bear coffee

Dairy Brand coffee

Golden Robin coffee

Honeymoon coffee

Wampum coffee

Forbes Golden Cup coffee

Turkey coffee

Jam-Boy coffee

IGA oats

Buffalo Brand peanuts

Welcome Guest coffee

American Lady coffee

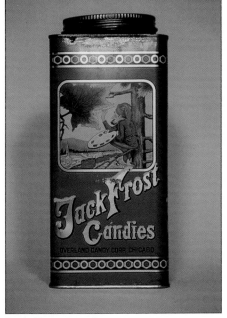

Jack Frost candy

Schrafft's candy

Mity-Good coffee

Dairy Brand coffee

Camp Fire coffee

Strong-Heart coffee

King Cole coffee

Jersey Cream coffee

Convention Hall coffee

Swansdown coffee

Kamargo coffee

Campfire marshmallows

Old City peanut butter

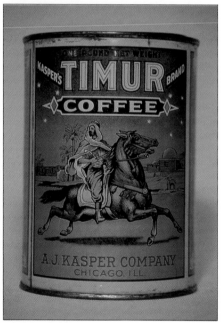

Timur coffee

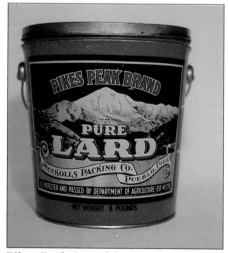

Pikes Peak Brand lard

Our Mother's, rectangular, cardboard, 9¼ × 4½ × 3½, **$25**

Our Mother's, round, cardboard, 10½ × 4½, **$25**

Monarch, square, lithograph, 5 × 2½ × 2½, **$50**

Monarch, square, lithograph, 3 × 1½ × 1½, **$40**

Pioneer, square, lithograph,
5½ × 4 × 4, **$50**

Rockwood, square, lithograph,
5 × 2½ × 2½, **$60**

Rock-Co, round, cardboard,
10½ × 4½, **$20**

Royal Scarlet, square, lithograph,
6 × 3 × 3, **$40**

Runkel Brothers, square, lithograph, 5 × 2½ × 2½, **$35**

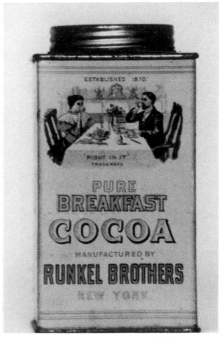

Runkel Brothers, square, lithograph, 5 × 2½ × 2½, **$65**

Royal Zest, square, lithograph, 5 × 4 × 4, **$65**

Rose's, square, lithograph, 5 × 2½ × 2½, **$60**

Triangle Club, square, lithograph,
5½ × 3½ × 3½, **$50**

Trueworth, rectangular, cardboard,
9½ × 5 × 3, **$35**

Wilbur Dutch, rectangular, paper
label, 6½ × 4 × 2, **$35**

Winner, square, lithograph,
6 × 3 × 3, **$35**

White City, rectangular, cardboard,
9½ × 5 × 3, **$35**

Stollwerck, odd, lithograph,
4 × 4 × 1, **$30**

Coconut

Gorton's, rectangular, lithograph,
4½ × 3¼ × 2, **$75**

Brunswick, square, lithograph,
5 × 2½ × 2½, **$60**

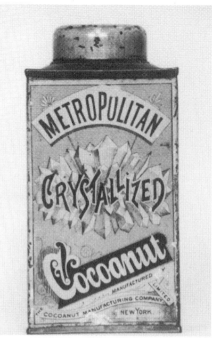

Metropolitan, square, lithograph,
5½ × 3 × 3, **$65**

Crystallized, round, lithograph,
5 × 3, **$50**

Maltby's, square, lithograph,
4 × 2½ × 2½, **$50**

Davis, John; square; lithograph;
4 × 2½ × 2½; **$50**

Hoyt's, square, lithograph,
4 × 2½ × 2½, **$65**

Metropolitan, square, lithograph,
4 × 2½ × 2½, **$65**

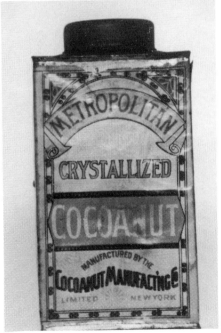

Metropolitan, square, paper label,
5½ × 3 × 3, **$50**

Maltby's, round, lithograph,
4½ × 3, **$60**

Windsor, square, paper label,
4 × 2½ × 2½, **$30**

Coffee

Advo, round, lithograph, 8½ × 6¼,
$35

Allpure, round, lithograph,
10¼ × 5½, **$200**

Advo, round, lithograph, 2½ × 3,
$35

After Dinner, pail, lithograph,
8 × 8, **$45**

Aladdin, round, lithograph,
5¼ × 4¼, **$30**

After Glow, pail, lithograph, 8 × 8,
$45

MacDougall, Alice Foote; round; lithograph; 6 × 4¼; **$50**

American Beauty, round, paper label, 6 × 4½, **$125**

American Home, round, paper label, 6 × 4½, **$45**

Ambero, round, paper label, 6 × 4½, **$65**

American Lady, round, lithograph,
5½ × 4½, **$150**

American Lady, round, lithograph,
9½ × 5½, **$200**

Anchor, round, lithograph,
4 × 5½, **$75**

Anona, rectangular, lithograph,
6 × 4½ × 3, **$45**

Arabian Banquet, round, lithograph, 9½ × 5½, **$300**

Astor House, round, lithograph,
5½ × 4½, **$75**

Atwood's, round, lithograph,
6 × 4¼, **$30**

Aunt Minerva, pail, lithograph,
7½ × 6, **$250**

37

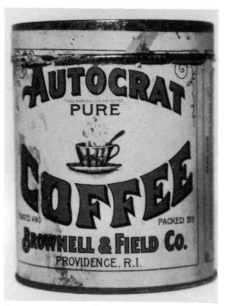

Autocrat, round, paper label,
5 × 4¼, **$40**

Baby Stuart, round, paper label,
6 × 4¼, **$65**

Avon Club, round, paper label,
5½ × 4¼, **$35**

Baker, round, paper label,
10 × 5½, **$100**

Bagdad, pail, lithograph, 9 × 7½, **$150**

Barrington Hall, round, lithograph, 6 × 4½, **$45**

Battleship, round, lithograph, 6 × 4, **$85**

Berma, round, lithograph, 6 × 4¼, **$35**

Berma, round, lithograph, 6 × 4¼,
$30

Bird, round, lithograph, 14 × 5,
$100

Best Value, round, paper label,
5½ × 4¼, **$35**

Beverly Club, round, paper label,
6 × 4, **$45**

Blanke's Happy Thought, rectangular, lithograph, 4½ × 9 × 5, **$60**

Biston's (sample), round, lithograph, 1½ × 3, **$25**

Blanke's Saratoga, rectangular, lithograph, 7 × 9 × 5, **$85**

Beech-Nut (sample), round, lithograph, 2½ × 3½, **$20**

Blanke's Saratoga, rectangular, lithograph, 7 × 9 × 5, **$75**

Big Horn, round, lithograph,
5½ × 4½, **$200**

Blackstone, round, lithograph,
9 × 6, **$95**

Blanke's Defy, pail, lithograph,
8½ × 7½, **$200**

Blanke's Oak Lawn, square, lithograph, 9 × 5 × 5, **$225**

Blanke's Jersey Cream, pail, lithograph, 9 × 5, **$175**

Blanke's Defy, pail, lithograph, 11 × 7½, **$250**

Blanke's Mojav, square, lithograph, 7½ × 5 × 5, **$75**

Blanke's Portonilla, pail, lithograph, 10 × 6, **$250**

Bliss, round, lithograph, 5¼ × 7, **$25**

Blue Flame, round, paper label, 3½ × 5½, **$30**

Blue Ribbon, round, lithograph, 4 × 5¼, **$35**

Blue Ribbon, round, lithograph, 7½ × 6½, **$75**

Briardale, round, lithograph, 3½ × 5½, **$10**

Breakfast Cheer (sample), round, lithograph, 2¼ × 2½, **$50**

Blanke's World's Fair, round, lithograph, 11 × 3½, **$200**

Blue Bird, round, lithograph, 9½ × 5½, **$125**

Brown Betty, round, lithograph, 10 × 5½, **$75**

Blue Bird, pail, lithograph, 7 × 6½, **$45**

Blue Flame, pail, lithograph, 8½ × 6, **$45**

Blue Grass Belle, round, paper label, 6 × 4½, **$100**

Bluhill, pail, lithograph, 10½ × 7½, **$125**

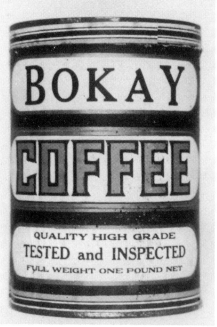

Bokay, round, paper label, 6 × 4, **$25**

Bokar, round, lithograph, 6 × 4,
$20

Bokar, round, lithograph, 6 × 4,
$25

Bouquet, round, lithograph,
5½ × 4¼, **$60**

Bouquet, rectangular, lithograph,
6½ × 4½ × 3¼, **$75**

Bouquet, rectangular, lithograph,
7 × 6 × 4, **$65**

Breakfast Call, round, lithograph,
9 × 6¼, **$50**

Breakfast Call, round, lithograph,
6 × 4¼, **$25**

Breakfast Call, round, lithograph,
6 × 4¼, **$40**

Brighton Blend, round, lithograph,
6 × 4¼, **$100**

Bridal Brand, oval, lithograph,
6 × 5 × 3, **$75**

Brownie, rectangular, paper label,
6 × 4½ × 3½, **$65**

Brown Thrush, round, paper label,
6 × 4¼, **$75**

Brundage, round, lithograph,
6 × 4¼, **$65**

Bunker Hill, round, lithograph,
6 × 4¼, **$65**

Bunny Blend, round, paper label,
6 × 4¼, **$150**

Cambridge, square, lithograph,
7 × 3½ × 3½, **$100**

Camo Brand, pail, lithograph,
8¼ × 7½, **$125**

Café Royale, round, paper label,
6 × 4½, **$100**

Bonnette, round, lithograph,
4 × 5¼, **$150**

Campbell, pail, lithograph, 8 × 8,
$60

Butter-Nut, round, paper label,
3¼ × 5½, **$20**

Butter-Nut, round, lithograph,
3 × 4, **$15**

Camp Fire, round, lithograph,
8 × 5½, **$400**

Capitol, pail, lithograph, 9 × 7½,
$100

Canton, rectangular, lithograph,
7 × 6 × 4, **$100**

Capitol Mills, round, lithograph,
5½ × 5, **$350**

Carnation, round, lithograph,
6 × 4, **$100**

Carnival, round, paper label,
5 × 4½, **$100**

Carnation Santos, round, lithograph, 8 × 5, **$100**

Carnation, round, paper label,
4 × 5¼, **$35**

Caswell's National Crest, round, lithograph, 7¼ × 5¼, **$35**

Caswell's Kona, round, lithograph, 7½ × 5½, **$35**

Caswell's, round, lithograph, 9 × 5½, **$85**

Cebu, round, paper label, 10 × 5½, **$45**

Old Time coffee

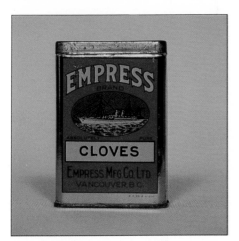

Empress spice

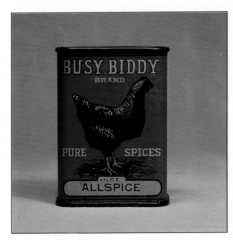

Busy Biddy spice

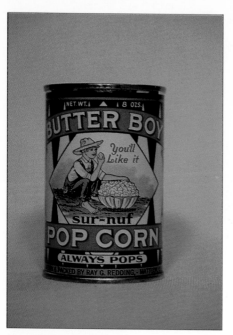

Butter Boy popcorn

Dove Brand spice

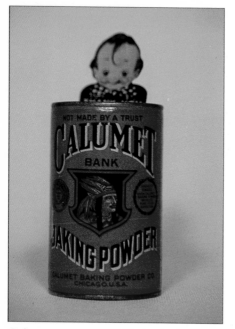

Calumet Bank baking powder

Little Elf coffee

Manor House coffee

Bob-White baking powder

Lakeland oats

Tiger oats

Sunshine crackers

Sunny Brook spice

Tuxedo spice

Conductor coffee

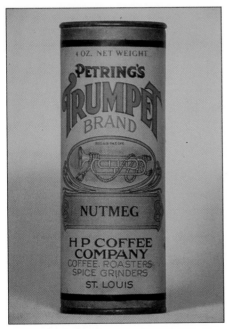

Trumpet spice

Slade's spice

Bell's spice

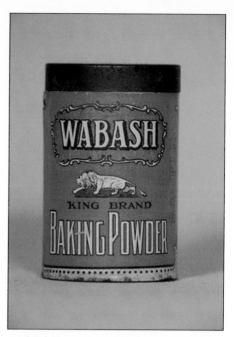

Wabash baking powder

Court House spice

Arm & Hammer baking soda

Bunker Hill coffee

Liberty Bond coffee

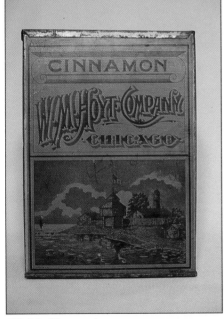

W. M. Hoyt spice

Hills Bros. coffee

Skookum syrup

Chase & Sanborn's, round, paper label, 5 × 4¼, **$25**

Chase & Sanborn's, round, paper label, 5 × 4½, **$25**

Central Market, rectangular, lithograph, 9 × 9 × 5¼, **$175**

Chase & Sanborn's, pail, lithograph, 10½ × 7½, **$125**

Chase & Sanborn, rectangular, paper label, 9½ × 9 × 4, **$100**

Charter Oak, round, paper label,
5 × 5, **$75**

Chocolate Cream, pail, paper label,
8 × 7½, **$30**

Chocolate Cream, cup, lithograph,
3 × 2¼, **$75**

Chase & Sanborn's (sample), round,
lithograph, 2 × 2½, **$45**

Chase & Sanborn's (sample), round,
lithograph, 2 × 2½, **$35**

Chocolate Cream, oval, paper label,
4¼ × 3, **$75**

Chocolate Cream, round, lithograph, 9 × 6¼, **$45**

Chocolate Cream, pail, lithograph,
10½ × 7½, **$85**

Chocolate Cream, round, lithograph, 6½ × 5, **$30**

Chocolate Cream, oval, paper label, 6½ × 4½, **$50**

Christy's, round, lithograph, 6 × 4, **$75**

Clover Farm, round, lithograph, 6½ × 5¼, **$35**

Chocolate Cream, round, lithograph, 4 × 5, **$20**

Chocolate Cream, round, paper label, 4 × 5½, **$35**

Commodore, pail, lithograph,
7 × 5½, **$200**

Colonial Dame, round, lithograph,
6 × 4¼, **$65**

Colonial Dame, pail, lithograph,
8¼ × 7½, **$125**

Clover Farm, round, lithograph,
3½ × 5½, **$20**

Colonial Hotel, square, lithograph,
6½ × 3½ × 3½, **$65**

Comrade, round, lithograph,
7½ × 6¼, **$65**

Colonial Inn, round, paper label,
5½ × 4½, **$65**

Comrade, round, lithograph, 8 × 5,
$400

Comrade, round, lithograph,
4 × 5¼, **$100**

Cool Roasted, round, lithograph,
3½ × 5, **$20**

Conductor, round, cardboard,
3½ × 5½, **$75**

Coronation Blend, round, lithograph, 6 × 4, **$45**

Convention Hall, round, lithograph,
6 × 4¼, **$250**

Corbin's, round, paper label,
6 × 4¼, **$50**

Council Oak, round, paper label,
5½ × 4¼, **$100**

Cream, pail, lithograph, 10½ × 7½,
$150

Daddy's Choice, round, lithograph,
5½ × 4½, **$300**

Co-op, pail, lithograph, 5½ × 6,
$30

Dairy Brand, pail, lithograph,
10½ × 7½, **$200**

Dairy Brand, pail, lithograph,
11 × 12, **$500**

Dairy Brand, pail, lithograph,
9 × 7½, **$170**

"Dainty," round, paper label,
5½ × 4¼, **$45**

Daisee, round, lithograph, 6 × 4¼,
$90

Dauntless, round, paper label,
6 × 4¼, **$75**

D. C. & H., round, lithograph,
6 × 4¼, **$55**

Deerwood, round, cardboard,
6 × 4, **$35**

Dilworth's, round, lithograph,
6 × 4¼, **$55**

Del Monte, round, lithograph,
3½ × 5, **$15**

Dells Extra, rectangular, paper label, 6 × 4¼ × 3¼, **$30**

Dilworth's (sample), round, lithograph, 2½ × 2, **$35**

Dinner Party, round, cardboard,
5½ × 4¼, **$30**

Dinner Party, pail, lithograph,
11 × 7½, **$175**

Donald Duck (sample), round, lithograph, 2½ × 3, **$200**

Dot (sample), round, lithograph,
2½ × 2, **$35**

Domino, round, paper label,
6 × 4¼, **$65**

Drako, round, lithograph, 6 × 4¼,
$150

Eagle, round, lithograph, 6 × 4,
$85

Eagle Brand, round, paper label,
5½ × 4¼, **$65**

Elephant, rectangular, lithograph, 5½ × 8 × 5½, **$200**

Elephant, pail, lithograph, 8 × 8,
$150

Edgemere Brand, rectangular, lithograph, 7 × 6 × 4, **$65**

Ekko, round, paper label, 6 × 4, **$50**

Empress, pail, lithograph, 9 × 7½, **$35**

Eureka, pail, lithograph, 6 × 5, **$250**

Excelsior, round, paper label, 6 × 4, **$45**

Fall-Leaf, round, lithograph,
6 × 4¼, **$60**

Fair Deal, round, paper label,
6 × 4¼, **$75**

Fairway, round, lithograph, 4 × 5,
$40

Fairy Dell, pail, lithograph, 8 × 7,
$35

Family Blend, pail, lithograph,
8 × 7, **$45**

Famous, round, paper label,
6 × 4¼, **$75**

F. B. G., round, cardboard,
3½ × 5½, **$25**

Festival, round, lithograph,
3½ × 5½, **$35**

Farma, round, paper label,
6¼ × 5½, **$65**

Flaroma, rectangular, cardboard,
6¼ × 5¼ × 3, **$30**

Folger's, round, lithograph,
6½ × 5, **$25**

Folger's, round, paper label,
8½ × 6, **$75**

Folger's, round, lithograph, 8 × 6,
$50

Foley's, pail, lithograph, 8½ × 6,
$50

Folger's, round, lithograph, 10 × 7,
$100

Folger's, round, lithograph,
3½ × 5½, **$15**

Forbes, round, lithograph,
3½ × 5½, **$35**

Foltz Maid, round, lithograph,
6 × 4¼, **$150**

Forbes Golden Cup, round, lithograph, 9½ × 6, **$85**

Forbes Martha Washington, round, lithograph, 4 × 5, **$45**

Fort Pitt, round, lithograph, 4 × 5, **$45**

Forbes, round, lithograph, 3½ × 5½, **$40**

Forbes, pail, lithograph, 5½ × 7½, **$45**

Forbes (sample), round, lithograph, 2¼ × 3, **$50**

Fort Pitt, round, lithograph,
5½ × 4½, **$100**

Fort Western, round, lithograph,
6 × 4¼, **$45**

Franklin, round, lithograph,
9½ × 6, **$800**

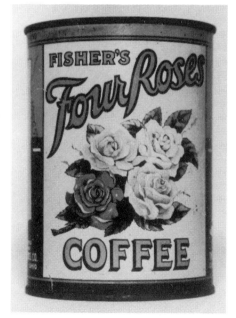

Four Roses, round, lithograph,
5½ × 4½, **$85**

French Opera, pail, lithograph,
7½ × 6¼, **$150**

Freshpak, round, lithograph,
6 × 4¼, **$50**

Frontier, round, lithograph,
4 × 5¼, **$100**

Garland, pail, lithograph, 11 × 7½,
$125

Gem of Boston, round, paper label,
6 × 4, **$50**

Gillies' Country Club, pail, lithograph, 11 × 7, **$50**

Glendora (sample), round, cardboard, 3¼ × 2, **$20**

Gold Bond, round, paper label,
5½ × 4¼, **$30**

Gold Cup, round, paper label,
6 × 4, **$50**

Gold Medal, round, lithograph,
6 × 4, **$40**

Gold Bond, round, lithograph,
4 × 5, **$30**

Gold Coast, round, lithograph,
6 × 4¼, **$50**

Golden Days, round, paper label,
6 × 4½, **$45**

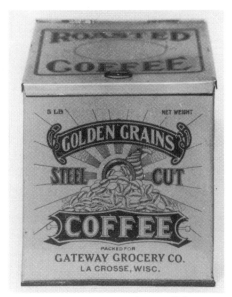

Golden Grains, slant front, lithograph, 9½ × 6½ × 7½, **$200**

Golden Robin, round, lithograph,
4 × 5½, **$200**

Golden Leaf, rectangular, cardboard, 6 × 4½ × 3, **$50**

Golden Rod, round, cardboard,
3½ × 5½, **$35**

Golden Sun, round, paper label,
5½ × 4½, **$45**

Golden West, round, lithograph,
6 × 5, **$35**

Golden Rod, round, paper label,
5 × 4¼, **$45**

Golden Sun, round, paper label,
10 × 6, **$50**

Goodhonest, round, lithograph,
5½ × 4½, **$200**

Golden West, round, lithograph,
7 × 6¼, **$65**

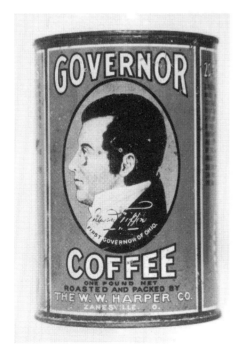

Governor, round, lithograph,
6 × 4¼, **$85**

Green Mountain, round, paper label, 6 × 4½, **$35**

Halligan's, round, lithograph,
9½ × 6, **$90**

Holland's, round, paper label,
5¼ × 4¼, **$35**

Hamill's, round, cardboard,
3½ × 5½, **$40**

Halligan's, round, lithograph,
6 × 4¼, **$30**

Harvest Home, round, lithograph,
3½ × 5½, **$25**

Hello World, round, paper label,
6 × 4½, **$45**

Hersh's Best, round, lithograph,
6 × 4¼, **$50**

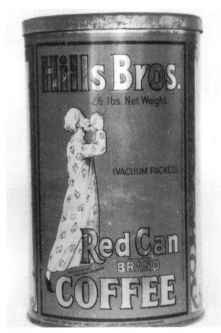

Hills Bros., round, lithograph,
8 × 5, **$50**

High Lindens, round, lithograph,
6 × 4¼, **$40**

Hills Bros., round, lithograph,
3½ × 5, **$45**

Hills Bros, round, lithograph,
3½ × 5, **$12**

Home Brand, round, lithograph,
3½ × 5½, **$15**

Honeymoon, round, lithograph,
6 × 7, **$125**

Honeymoon Trail, round, lithograph, 4 × 5¼, **$300**

H. & R. (sample), round, lithograph, 2 × 2½, **$30**

Holland House, round, lithograph, 6 × 4¼, **$45**

Hood's, round, lithograph, 6 × 4, **$35**

Home Brand, pail, lithograph, 9 × 7½, **$50**

Hoosier Boy, round, paper label, 6 × 4½, **$175**

Hostess, round, lithograph,
6 × 4½, **$30**

Hotel McAlpin, square, lithograph,
10 × 6 × 6, **$75**

Huntoon, Paige; rectangular; lithograph; 7 × 6 × 4; **$100**

Ideal Blend, round, paper label,
5 × 4¼, **$35**

Ideal, round, lithograph, 6 × 4¼,
$45

Illinois Club, round, lithograph,
10¼ × 5½, **$75**

Imperio, round, lithograph, 9 × 5,
$50

Ivanhoe, rectangular, lithograph,
5¼ × 6 × 4, **$45**

Inca Maiden, pail, lithograph,
7½ × 7½, **$200**

Jack Sprat, pail, lithograph,
8 × 7½, **$300**

Jack Sprat, round, cardboard,
4½ × 5, **$100**

Jack Sprat, round, paper label,
7¼ × 5¼, **$75**

J. M. 1846, round, lithograph,
4 × 5½, **$35**

Jam-Boy, round, paper label,
6 × 4½, **$125**

Jam-Boy, round, lithograph,
5½ × 4½, **$175**

Jersey Cream, pail, lithograph,
10½ × 7½, **$250**

Jenny Wren, round, paper label,
5½ × 4½, **$100**

Kaffee Hag, round, lithograph,
6 × 4¼, **$30**

Kaffee Hag, square, cardboard,
6½ × 3½ × 3½, **$25**

Kaffee Hag (sample), round, lithograph, 2 × 2½, **$50**

Kamargo, round, lithograph,
5½ × 4½, **$150**

Kar-A-Van, round, lithograph,
5 × 4¼, **$45**

King Cole, round, lithograph,
6 × 4¼, **$200**

Kingfisher, pail, lithograph,
7½ × 7½, **$150**

King Cole, round, lithograph,
3 × 4¼, **$125**

Kellams Little Giant, round, paper label, 5½ × 4¼, **$50**

Kleeko, round, lithograph, 6 × 4½, **$45**

Kenny's Hotel Brand, round, lithograph, 8 × 7½, **$200**

Kenny's Maid, pail, lithograph, 8 × 7½, **$170**

Ko-Zee Inn, round, paper label,
5½ × 4¼, **$45**

Kybo, round, lithograph, 6 × 4¼,
$35

Lady Baltimore, round, paper label,
6 × 4½, **$85**

Lady Hellen, round, paper label,
6 × 4½, **$65**

La Touraine, round, paper label,
6 × 4, **$30**

Lidco, round, lithograph, 6 × 4½,
$45

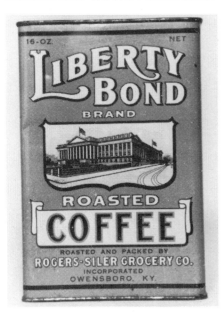

Liberty Bond, rectangular, lithograph, 6¼ × 4¼ × 3, **$45**

Lee, round, lithograph, 4 × 5½,
$45

Lion, round, lithograph, 3½ × 5,
$50

Light House, round, paper label,
6 × 4, **$65**

Light House, round, paper label,
5½ × 4¼, **$85**

Lily of the Valley, round, lithograph, 6 × 4¼, **$75**

Liner, round, paper label,
5½ × 4½, **$75**

Lipton's, round, paper label,
5½ × 4¼, **$25**

Lipton's, round, lithograph,
6 × 4¼, **$40**

Little Elf, round, lithograph,
6 × 4¼, **$75**

Locomotive 999, round, paper label, 6 × 4½, **$125**

Louis, round, lithograph,
10¼ × 5½, **$200**

Loyl, round, lithograph, 6 × 4¼,
$85

Louis, round, lithograph, 4 × 5¼,
$100

Madura, round, lithograph,
6 × 4½, **$85**

Luzianne, round, lithograph,
6 × 4¼, **$35**

Luzianne, round, paper label,
5 × 4¼, **$35**

Manru (sample), round, lithograph,
2½ × 2, **$30**

Luzianne, pail, lithograph, 8 × 6½,
$45

Manhattan, round, lithograph,
4 × 5, **$35**

Manor House, round, cardboard, 6 × 4, **$45**

Massasoit, round, paper label, 5 × 4¼, **$100**

Martinson's, round, lithograph, 4 × 5, **$30**

Maryland Club (sample), round, lithograph, 2¼ × 2, **$25**

Matchless, round, lithograph, 6 × 4¼, **$50**

Maxwell House, round, lithograph,
6 × 5, **$25**

May-Day, round, paper label,
4 × 5½, **$25**

Maxwell House, round, lithograph,
4 × 5½, **$25**

Maxwell House, round, lithograph,
6 × 5, **$20**

Maxwell House (sample), round,
lithograph, 1½ × 2, **$20**

Maxwell House, round, lithograph,
3½ × 5½, **$15**

Maxwell House, round, paper label,
6 × 4, **$45**

Maxwell House, round, lithograph,
6½ × 5, **$25**

Maxwell House, round, lithograph,
5 × 5, **$25**

Maxwell House, round, lithograph,
4 × 5¼, **$15**

McFadden's, round, paper label,
3½ × 5½, **$35**

McLaughlin's, round, lithograph,
5 × 8, **$45**

McLaughlin's, round, lithograph,
4¼ × 5¼, **$35**

Millar's, round, lithograph,
3½ × 5½, **$25**

Mi-Lady, round, lithograph,
5½ × 4½, **$300**

Military, round, lithograph,
4 × 5¼, **$100**

McLaughlin's, round, lithograph,
6 × 4½, **$65**

McLaughlin's, round, lithograph,
7 × 6, **$75**

Millar's, round, paper label,
10 × 5½, **$45**

Millar, E. B.; round; paper label;
6½ × 5½; **$45**

Millar's, round, paper label,
6 × 4¼, **$35**

M-J-B, round, lithograph,
8½ × 5½, **$30**

M-J-B, round, lithograph,
2½ × 4¼, **$25**

Mocha & Java, rectangular, lithograph, 7 × 6 × 4, **$65**

Mocha & Java, round, paper label, 5½ × 4¼, **$25**

Mity-Good, rectangular, cardboard, 6 × 4½ × 3¼, **$200**

Mocha and Java, round, paper label, 6½ × 4, **$100**

Mocha and Java, square, lithograph, 7 × 5½ × 5½, **$100**

Mohican, round, lithograph,
5½ × 4½, **$100**

Monadnock, round, lithograph,
6 × 4¼, **$50**

Mocha and Java, rectangular, lithograph, 7 × 6 × 4, **$100**

Monarch, round, lithograph,
5½ × 4½, **$75**

Montana Maid, round, paper label,
6 × 4, **$85**

Mount Cross, round, lithograph,
8 × 6½, **$45**

Morning Glow, round, lithograph,
6 × 4, **$55**

Mount Cross, round, lithograph,
4 × 5¼, **$45**

Morning Sip, round, lithograph,
5½ × 4¼, **$45**

Morton House, round, lithograph,
6 × 4¼, **$35**

Nash's (sample), round, paper label,
2 × 3¼, **$50**

Nash's, round, lithograph,
3½ × 5½, **$15**

Morey Mills, rectangular, lithograph, 8 × 6 × 3; **$100**

Nash's, pail, lithograph, 9 × 7½, **$65**

Nash's, round, paper label, 5½ × 4, **$20**

Nash's, round, lithograph, 6½ × 5, **$30**

Nescafé (sample), round, lithograph, 2¼ × 1¼, **$20**

Old Colony, round, paper label,
6 × 4, **$45**

Old Colony, round, paper label,
6 × 4, **$65**

Old Judge, round, lithograph,
3½ × 5½, **$15**

Oak Hill, round, lithograph,
6 × 4¼, **$65**

Old Master, round, lithograph,
6 × 4, **$75**

Old Master, round, lithograph,
6 × 4½, **$65**

Old Judge, round, lithograph,
10¼ × 5½, **$125**

Old Judge (sample), round, lithograph, 2½ × 3, **$45**

Old Southern, round, lithograph,
5½ × 4½, **$100**

Old Time, round, lithograph,
10 × 5½, **$150**

Old Time, round, lithograph,
4 × 5¼, **$85**

Olive Branch, rectangular, cardboard, 6¼ × 4¼ × 3¼, **$45**

Our Best Drips, round, paper label,
4½ × 3½, **$65**

Our Pride, pail, lithograph,
8½ × 7½, **$100**

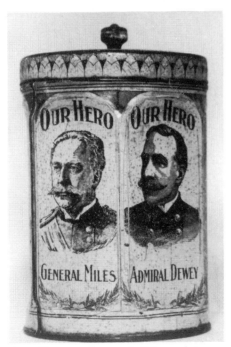

Our Hero, octagonal, lithograph,
6 × 4, **$300**

Our Standard, round, paper label,
7½ × 4¼, **$150**

Pacific, round, lithograph, 7½ × 5, **$85**

Pickwick, round, lithograph, 8 × 6, **$75**

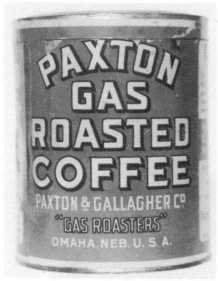

Paxton, round, paper label, 6½ × 5½, **$45**

Pickwick, round, lithograph, 4 × 5¼, **$35**

Par, round, lithograph, 4 × 5¼, **$15**

Parke's, round, lithograph,
9¼ × 7½, **$250**

Peak, round, lithograph, 6 × 4¼,
$25

Pilot-Knob, round, paper label,
5½ × 4¼, **$35**

Pilot-Knob, pail, lithograph,
9 × 7½, **$55**

Pathfinder, round, paper label,
4 × 5½, **$35**

Princess Patt, round, lithograph,
3½ × 5½, **$45**

Polar Bear, round, lithograph,
3½ × 5, **$45**

Red Rose, round, cardboard,
4 × 5½, **$25**

Red Rose, round, lithograph,
4 × 5¼, **$35**

Red Trail, round, paper label,
3½ × 5½, **$45**

Planters House, round, lithograph,
5½ × 4½, **$150**

Plee-zing, round, lithograph,
10 × 5½, **$50**

Quezal, rectangular, lithograph,
2¼ × 6 × 4, **$75**

Red Wolf, pail, lithograph, 9¼ × 8,
$125

Red Turkey, round, lithograph,
6 × 4¼, **$150**

Revere, round, paper label,
5 × 4¼, **$100**

Red Wolf, round, lithograph,
4 × 5¼, **$75**

Richelieu, round, paper label,
5½ × 4¼, **$30**

Richelieu (sample), round, lithograph, 2½ × 2, **$50**

Rose Bud, rectangular, paper label, 3½ × 6 × 4, **$45**

Rivera, pail, lithograph, 11 × 7½,
$150

Right Hand, round, paper label,
6 × 4¼, **$65**

Roof Garden, round, lithograph, 5¼ × 4¼, **$30**

Rosy Morn, pail, lithograph, 8 × 7½, **$65**

Riverside Club, round, paper label, 3½ × 5½, **$45**

"Royal" (sample), round, lithograph, 3 × 2, **$35**

Royal Blue Stores, round, lithograph, 5 × 4¼, **$30**

Royal Corona, round, lithograph, 11½ × 10, **$50**

Royal Quality, pail, lithograph, 9 × 7½, **$50**

Royal M, round, lithograph, 6 × 4¼, **$50**

Royal Peach, round, paper label, 6 × 4¼, **$45**

Sally Clover, round, lithograph,
6 × 4¼, **$40**

Ruby, pail, lithograph, 5½ × 4¼,
$85

Santa Fe Trail, round, paper label,
4 × 5¼, **$100**

Sanka, round, lithograph,
3½ × 5½, **$15**

Sky Maid, round, lithograph,
3½ × 5½, **$50**

San Marto, round, lithograph,
5½ × 4½, **$75**

Seminole, square, paper label,
9 × 5 × 5, **$100**

Scarlet King, oval, paper label,
6½ × 4½, **$125**

Seal Brand, round, paper label,
5 × 4½, **$30**

Silver Moon, round, paper label, 6 × 4½, **$75**

Silver Sea, round, lithograph, 6 × 4¼, **$35**

Senate, round, lithograph, 6 × 4¼, **$75**

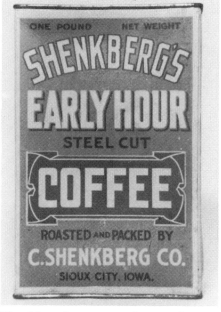

Shenkberg's, rectangular, card-board, 6½ × 4½ × 3, **$45**

Smith, Gage; square; lithograph;
8 × 5 × 5; **$85**

Splendora, round, paper label,
6 × 4¼, **$100**

Special Combination, pail, lithograph, 10 × 10, **$75**

Stewarts, round, lithograph,
3½ × 5, **$20**

St. Elmo, pail, lithograph, 8 × 7½, **$45**

Shapleigh's, round, paper label, 6 × 5½, **$45**

State House, round, cardboard, 5½ × 4¼, **$65**

Strong-Heart, round, lithograph, 5½ × 4½, **$300**

Stone's, pail, lithograph, 9 × 7½, **$35**

Summer Girl, round, lithograph, 4 × 5½, **$35**

Sun Flower, round, lithograph, 4 × 5¼, **$100**

Sunshine, round, lithograph, 3½ × 5½, **$30**

Suprex, round, lithograph, 4 × 5½, **$18**

Suprex, round, lithograph, 4 × 5½, **$18**

Swansdown, round, lithograph,
6 × 4¼, **$75**

Sweet Melody, round, paper label,
6½ × 4, **$50**

Tac-Cut, round, lithograph,
6 × 4¼, **$175**

Ten Eyck, round, lithograph,
8 × 6, **$75**

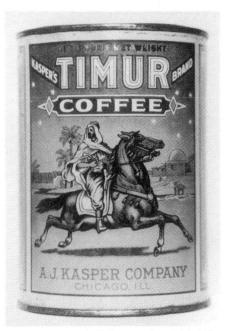

Timur, round, lithograph, 6 × 4½,
$300

Tone's, round, paper label,
5½ × 4¼, **$25**

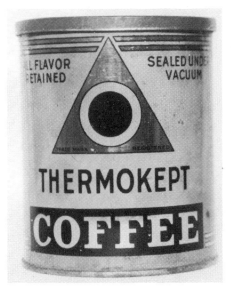

Thermokept, round, lithograph,
5 × 4½, **$30**

Tone's, round, lithograph, 3½ × 5,
$20

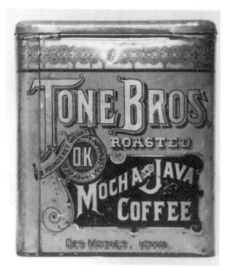

Tone Bros., rectangular, lithograph, 7 × 6 × 4, **$65**

Tone Bros, pail, lithograph, 8 × 8,
$65

Tower, round, paper label,
5½ × 4¼, **$65**

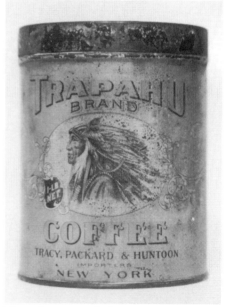

Trapahu, round, lithograph,
6 × 4¼, **$150**

Turkey, round, lithograph,
10½ × 5½, **$175**

Universal, round, lithograph,
8 × 6, **$200**

Turkey, round, lithograph,
5½ × 4½, **$150**

Tudor, round, paper label, 5 × 4¼,
$35

Union Club, round, paper label,
5½ × 4¼, **$35**

Union Club, round, lithograph,
6 × 4¼, **$75**

Veteran Brand, round, lithograph,
5½ × 4½, **$100**

Veteran Brand, round, paper label,
6 × 4, **$85**

Wak-Em Up, pail, lithograph,
13 × 9, **$350**

Wak-Em Up, pail, lithograph,
9 × 7½, **$150**

Wak-Em-Up, round, cardboard,
3½ × 5½, **$65**

Vienna, round, lithograph, 3 × 3,
$35

Wampum, round, lithograph,
9¼ × 5½, **$150**

Wampum, round, paper label,
6 × 4½, **$100**

Ward, rectangular, cardboard,
6¼ × 5¼ × 3, **$30**

Warrior, square, lithograph,
7 × 5 × 5, **$100**

G Washington's, round, lithograph,
6½ × 4¼, **$50**

G. Washington's, round, lithograph,
5 × 3, **$15**

G. Washington's, round, lithograph,
3½ × 2½, **$18**

G Washington's, round, paper label,
3 × 2½, **$18**

W G Y, round, lithograph, 6 × 4¼, **$40**

Welcome Guest, round, lithograph, 6 × 4½, **$500**

Wellman (sample), round, lithograph, 2 × 2¼, **$40**

Webb, Thomas J.; round; lithograph; 9½ × 5½; **$50**

144

White Bear, rectangular, cardboard, 6 × 4½ × 3, **$45**

White Horse, round, cardboard, 6 × 4½, **$100**

White House (sample), round, lithograph, 3 × 2, **$75**

White Rose, round, lithograph, 6 × 4, **$35**

White Villa, round, lithograph, 4 × 5½, **$90**

White Way, round, cardboard,
6 × 4¼, **$75**

Wigwam, round, lithograph,
6 × 4½, **$90**

Wish Bone, pail, lithograph, 8 × 8,
$45

Wish Bone, round, lithograph,
7½ × 5, **$35**

Wonder, round, lithograph,
6½ × 5¼, **$25**

Wood's, round, paper label, 6 × 4,
$65

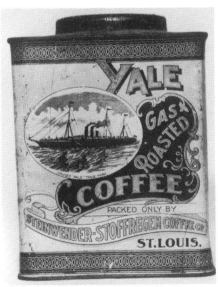

Yale, square, lithograph,
6 × 5 × 5, **$70**

Worthweil, round, lithograph,
5½ × 4¼, **$35**

Yale, round, lithograph, 8¼ × 6½, **$85**

Yale, round, lithograph, 6 × 4¼, **$75**

Yar, pail, lithograph, 8 × 7½, **$250**

Yale, round, lithograph, 7¼ × 5½, **$70**

6 O'Clock, round, lithograph,
6 × 4, **$60**

18-K, round, paper label, 7 × 5¼,
$30

Yellow Bonnet, round, lithograph,
3½ × 5½, **$30**

Yellow Bonnet, round, lithograph,
2½ × 3, **$125**

5th Ave, round, lithograph,
6 × 4¼, **$45**

Gum
and
Candy

Jack Frost, square, lithograph,
10 × 4½ × 4½, **$65**

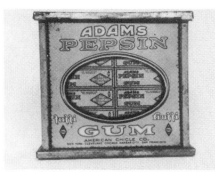

Adams, rectangular, lithograph,
6 × 7 × 5, **$125**

Adams, rectangular, lithograph,
6 × 7 × 5, **$200**

Adams, rectangular, lithograph,
6 × 7 × 5, **$200**

Beech-Nut, rectangular, lithograph,
3½ × 5¼ × 5, **$20**

Girl and Boat, pail, lithograph,
2½ × 4½ × 2½, **$40**

Monarch, round, lithograph,
3½ × 5, **$55**

Blome's, round, lithograph,
9 × 5½, **$30**

Bunte Diana, round, lithograph,
10 × 5½, **$30**

McDowell, Pyle; round; lithograph;
7 × 6; **$15**

Halloween, round, lithograph,
2 × 4, **$30**

Monarch, round, lithograph,
14½ × 12½, **$200**

Mad Tea-Party, round, lithograph,
2½ × 6, **$75**

Mother Goose, pail, lithograph,
2½ × 4½ × 2½, **$85**

Mother Goose, pail, lithograph,
3¼ × 4½ × 3¼, **$75**

Morses, square, lithograph,
10 × 5 × 5, **$65**

Peter Rabbit, oval, lithograph, 2½ × 4½ × 2½, **$85**

Peter Rabbit, round, lithograph, 2 × 4, **$50**

Peter Rabbit, pail, lithograph, 4¼ × 3 × 3, **$45**

Peter Rabbit, pail, lithograph, 2½ × 4½ × 2½, **$85**

Rabbits and Bears, rectangular, lithograph, 3¼ × 6 × 4, **$95**

Society Mints, round, lithograph,
10 × 8, **$40**

Schrafft's, round, lithograph,
5¼ × 3, **$100**

Yucatan, rectangular, lithograph,
6 × 7 × 5, **$100**

Marshmallows

Lily of the Valley, round, lithograph, 3½ × 5½, **$30**

Angelus, round, lithograph, 2½ × 7, **$75**

Angelus, round, paper label, 2 × 4, **$65**

Apollo, round, lithograph, 2 × 4, **$20**

Beich's, round, lithograph, 2 × 4, **$20**

Blue Bird, triangle, lithograph, 4 × 6 × 6, **$50**

Campfire, round, lithograph, 6 × 10, **$35**

Bunte, round, lithograph, 2¼ × 9, **$135**

Campfire, round, lithograph, 3½ × 6, **$75**

Campfire, round, lithograph, 2¼ × 9, **$45**

Cook Book, round, lithograph,
4 × 5½, **$65**

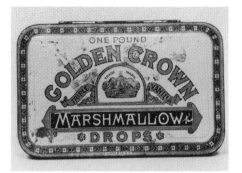

Golden Crown, rectangular, lithograph, 2½ × 6 × 4, **$25**

Everybody's, round, lithograph,
2 × 4, **$30**

Golden Pheasant, round, lithograph, 2 × 4, **$30**

Jack Sprat, round, paper label,
8 × 12½, **$50**

Kehoe, rectangular, lithograph,
2½ × 6 × 4, **$20**

Liberty, round, lithograph, 2 × 4,
$20

Log Cabin, round, lithograph,
6 × 10, **$75**

Newly Wed, round, lithograph,
2 × 4, **$35**

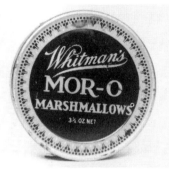

Mor-O, round, lithograph, 2 × 4,
$20

Patrician, round, lithograph, 2 × 4,
$20

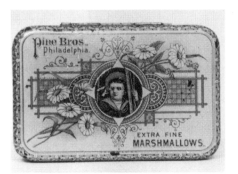

Pine Bros., rectangular, lithograph,
2½ × 6 × 4, **$40**

Shotwell's, round, lithograph,
3½ × 5½, **$50**

Prize Medal, round, lithograph,
2 × 4, **$30**

Sterling, round, lithograph, 6 × 10, **$45**

Rudd's, round, lithograph, 2 × 4,
$30

Superfine, oval, lithograph,
2½ × 4, **$20**

Sunset, round, lithograph, 2 × 4,
$30

Super Extra, rectangular, lithograph, 3½ × 6 × 4, **$30**

Super-Extra, rectangular, lithograph, 2½ × 6 × 4, **$50**

Swansdown, round, lithograph,
2 × 4, **$35**

Telmo, round, paper label,
3½ × 5½, **$35**

Yacht Club, round, cardboard,
3½ × 6, **$35**

Yacht Club, round, lithograph,
6 × 10, **$40**

Oats

Aunt Sally, round, cardboard,
8 × 5, **$25**

Armour's, round, cardboard,
7¼ × 4¼, **$25**

Baby Bunting, round, cardboard,
9 × 5, **$75**

Banner, round, cardboard,
9½ × 5½, **$18**

Builders, round, cardboard,
9½ × 5½, **$20**

Blue Ribbon, round, cardboard,
9½ × 5½, **$20**

Bonnie, round, cardboard,
9½ × 5½, **$25**

Briardale, round, cardboard,
9½ × 5½, **$18**

Castle, round, cardboard,
9½ × 5½, **$22**

Chippewa Shield, round, cardboard,
9½ × 5½, **$35**

Clover Farm, round, cardboard,
9½ × 5½, **$18**

D-B, round, cardboard, 9½ × 5½,
$14

Ecco, round, paper label, 9½ × 5½,
$24

Crystal Wedding, round, cardboard,
6 × 5, **$15**

Fairway, round, cardboard,
9½ × 5½, **$40**

Fargo, round, cardboard,
9½ × 5½, **$18**

Fi-Na-St, round, cardboard,
9½ × 5½, **$22**

Fort Dearborn, round, cardboard,
9½ × 5½, **$35**

Grand Union, round, cardboard,
9½ × 5½, **$30**

Hoffmann's, round, cardboard,
9½ × 5½, **$14**

Home Brand, round, cardboard,
9½ × 5½, **$25**

Indian, round, cardboard,
9½ × 5½, **$75**

Jack Sprat, round, cardboard,
7¼ × 4¼, **$50**

IGA, round, cardboard, 9½ × 5½,
$30

Joannes, round, cardboard,
9½ × 5½, **$15**

Kamo, round, cardboard,
7¼ × 4¼, **$75**

Lakeland, round, cardboard,
9½ × 5½, **$40**

Me Too, round, cardboard,
9½ × 5½, **$15**

Mother's, round, cardboard,
7¼ × 4¼, **$20**

Nation-Wide, round, cardboard,
9½ × 5½, **$20**

N. J. C., round, cardboard,
9½ × 5½, **$25**

Nicolet, round, cardboard,
9½ × 5½, **$75**

Pettijohn's, round, cardboard,
7¼ × 4¼, **$30**

Opal, round, cardboard, 9½ × 5½, **$30**

Plu-Nel, round, cardboard, 9½ × 5½, **$20**

Pride of Ohio, round, cardboard, 9½ × 5½, **$75**

Purity, round, cardboard, 6½ × 4, **$25**

Quaker, round, cardboard,
9½ × 5½, **$15**

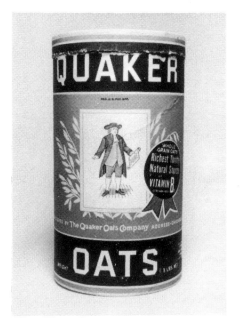

Quaker, round, cardboard,
9½ × 5½, **$15**

Quaker, round, cardboard,
9½ × 5½, **$15**

Red Mill, round, cardboard,
9½ × 5½, **$30**

Red & White, round, cardboard,
7¼ × 4¼, **$25**

Shryack, round, cardboard,
9½ × 5½, **$18**

Simon Pure, round, cardboard,
9½ × 5½, **$20**

Scotch Brand, round, cardboard,
9½ × 5½, **$20**

Sunnyfield, round, cardboard, 9½ × 5½, **$20**

Tiger, round, cardboard, 9½ × 5½, **$75**

Symns, round, cardboard, 9½ × 5½, **$22**

Ube See, round, cardboard, 9½ × 5½, **$15**

Wonder Ware, round, cardboard,
7¼ × 4¼, **$20**

Wonder Ware, round, cardboard,
6¼ × 4, **$20**

Yankee, round, cardboard,
9½ × 5½, **$75**

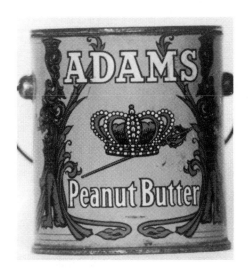

Peanut Butter

Adams, pail, lithograph, 3 × 4,
$250

Battleship, pail, lithograph,
3 × 3½, **$75**

Bayle, pail, lithograph, 3 × 3½, **$60**

Armour's, pail, lithograph, 3½ × 3,
$75

Aunt Sally, pail, lithograph,
3 × 3½, **$75**

Bayle, pail, lithograph, 3 × 4, **$60**

Beaver Brand, pail, lithograph,
3 × 4, **$400**

Bel-Car-Mo, round, lithograph,
3 × 4, **$50**

Bengal Brand, pail, lithograph,
3 × 4, **$175**

Bowes, pail, lithograph, 3 × 3½,
$50

Brownie, pail, lithograph, 3 × 3,
$100

Bishop's, round, lithograph, 5 × 3,
$50

Browne's, pail, lithograph, 3½ × 4,
$100

Buffalo Brand, pail, lithograph,
2½ × 4, **$50**

Capitol Brand, pail, lithograph,
2½ × 4, **$100**

Chef, round, lithograph, 4 × 3½,
$60

Climax, round, lithograph, 2½ × 4,
$50

C. P. C., pail, lithograph, 3 × 4,
$190

Chef, round, lithograph, 4 × 3¼, **$300**

Credo, pail, lithograph, 3 × 3½, **$35**

Cream, pail, lithograph, 3 × 3½, **$45**

Dixie, pail, lithograph, 3 × 3½, **$45**

Fi-Na-St, pail, lithograph, 3 × 3½, **$45**

Frontier, pail, lithograph, 3 × 3½, **$35**

G. D. M., pail, lithograph, 3 × 3½, **$50**

Gold Medal, round, lithograph, 3 × 3½, **$45**

Happy Home, round, lithograph, 2½ × 4, **$350**

Happy Home, pail, lithograph, 2½ × 4, **$375**

Hoppingtot Brand, pail, lithograph, 3 × 4, **$400**

Jackie Coogan, pail, lithograph, 3½ × 3, **$250**

Gold Flake, pail, lithograph, 3 × 3½, **$35**

Home Brand, pail, lithograph, 3 × 3½, **$100**

Hoody's, pail, lithograph, 3 × 4, **$175**

Jackie Coogan, pail, lithograph, 3 × 3, **$250**

Kamo, round, lithograph, 3 × 3½,
$100

Jackie Coogan, pail, lithograph,
3 × 3, **$250**

Jumbo, pail, lithograph, 3 × 3½,
$25

Jack Sprat, round, lithograph,
12 × 9, **$250**

Jack Sprat, pail, lithograph, 3 × 4,
$400

Kibbe's, pail, lithograph, 3 × 3½,
$40

Louis, pail, lithograph, 3 × 3½,
$100

Kidd's, pail, lithograph, 3 × 3,
$250

Kings, pail, lithograph, 3 × 3½,
$60

Light House, pail, lithograph,
3 × 4, **$100**

Larkin, pail, lithograph, 3 × 3½,
$40

Liner, pail, lithograph, 3 × 4, **$200**

Maxie Cobb, round, lithograph,
3 × 3½, **$300**

Max-I-Mum, round, lithograph,
3 × 4, **$100**

Maple Leaf, pail, lithograph, 3 × 4,
$50

Meadow-Sweet, pail, lithograph,
3 × 4, **$75**

Monarch, round, lithograph, 4 × 3,
$100

Monarch, pail, lithograph, 3 × 4,
$125

Marwin, pail, lithograph, 3 × 3,
$50

Monadnock, pail, lithograph,
3 × 3½, **$60**

Miller & Hart, round, lithograph,
2½ × 4, **$45**

Monopole, pail, lithograph, 3 × 4,
$50

Mosemann's, pail, lithograph,
4 × 2½, **$45**

Mosemann's, pail, lithograph,
3 × 3½, **$65**

Nash's, cup, lithograph, 2½ × 3,
$75

Niagara, pail, lithograph, 3 × 4,
$90

Nor Va, pail, lithograph, 3 × 4,
$50

Old City, pail, lithograph, 3 × 3½,
$125

Old Reliable, pail, lithograph,
3 × 3½, **$40**

Ontario, pail, lithograph, 3 × 4,
$125

Morris', pail, lithograph, 3 × 3½,
$150

O! Boy, pail, lithograph, 3 × 4,
$150

Ox-Heart, pail, lithograph, 3 × 4,
$50

Oz, round, lithograph, 8 × 4, **$15**

Palmetto, pail, lithograph, 3 × 3½, **$65**

Pallas, pail, lithograph, 3 × 3½, **$60**

Palmetto, round, lithograph, 3 × 4, **$50**

Pet, pail, lithograph, 3 × 4, **$175**

Peter Rabbit, round, lithograph, 2 × 4, **$600**

Peter Rabbit, pail, lithograph, 3 × 3½, **$200**

Premier, pail, lithograph, 3 × 4, **$50**

Peter Pan, round, lithograph, 2 × 4, **$45**

Peter Pan, round, lithograph, 1½ × 2, **$45**

Red Robin, pail, lithograph,
3 × 3½, **$150**

Red Seal, pail, lithograph, 3 × 3½,
$40

Punch, round, lithograph, 2 × 3½,
$50

Rayo, pail, lithograph, 3 × 3½, **$45**

Red Feather, pail, lithograph,
3 × 3½, **$250**

Red and White, pail, lithograph,
3 × 3½, **$50**

Roof Garden, pail, lithograph,
3 × 3½, **$100**

Santa Fe, round, lithograph,
2½ × 4, **$500**

Rival, pail, lithograph, 3 × 3½, **$60**

Royal Club, pail, lithograph,
2½ × 4, **$200**

School Boy, round, lithograph,
2½ × 4, **$60**

School Days, pail, lithograph,
3 × 4, **$125**

School Boy, pail, lithograph,
2½ × 4, **$250**

Silver Buckle, round, lithograph,
3 × 3½, **$35**

"Squirrel," round, lithograph,
3 × 4, **$100**

Skippy, round, lithograph, 3 × 3,
$100

"Squirrel," pail, lithograph, 3 × 3,
$100

Sultana, pail, lithograph, 3 × 4, **$90**

Sultana, pail, lithograph, 3 × 4, **$30**

St. Laurent's, pail, lithograph,
3 × 3½, **$50**

Squirrel, pail, lithograph, 3 × 4,
$100

Sunny Boy, pail, lithograph,
3 × 3½, **$75**

"Sweetheart," pail, lithograph,
3 × 3½, **$50**

Sweet Girl, pail, lithograph,
2½ × 4, **$400**

Toyland, pail, lithograph, 3 × 4,
$80

Teddie, pail, lithograph, 3 × 3½,
$200

Triangle Club, round, lithograph,
3 × 4, **$65**

Teddy Bear, pail, lithograph,
2½ × 4, **$500**

Upton's, pail, lithograph, 3 × 4,
$75

Try Me, pail, lithograph, 3 × 3, **$200**

Try-Me, pail, lithograph, 3 × 3½, **$50**

Veteran Brand, pail, lithograph, 3 × 3½, **$95**

Virginia's Pride, pail, lithograph, 3 × 3½, **$65**

Wapello Chief, pail, lithograph, 3 × 4, **$300**

Wellman Foods, round, lithograph, 3 × 4, **$65**

Tropical, pail, lithograph,
3½ × 4½, **$100**

Wigwam, pail, lithograph, 3 × 4,
$250

White Swan, pail, lithograph,
3 × 4, **$250**

Yorkshire Farm, pail, lithograph,
3 × 3½, **$125**

Yankee, pail, lithograph, 3 × 3½,
$50

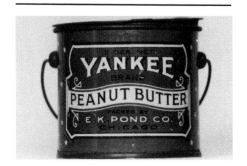

Wilson's, pail, lithograph, 3 × 3½, **$150**

Yellowstone, pail, lithograph, 3 × 3½, **$75**

Peanuts

Blue Moon, round, lithograph,
$11 \times 7\frac{1}{2}$, **$100**

After Dinner, round, lithograph,
9½ × 8, **$60**

Brownie, round, lithograph,
9½ × 8, **$75**

Buffalo Brand, round, lithograph,
9½ × 8, **$95**

Buddy, round, lithograph,
8½ × 8½, **$150**

Bunte, round, lithograph,
11¼ × 7½, **$100**

Elephant, round, lithograph,
11¼ × 7½, **$70**

Cream Dove, round, lithograph,
10 × 8, **$75**

Jumbo, round, lithograph, 9½ × 8,
$50

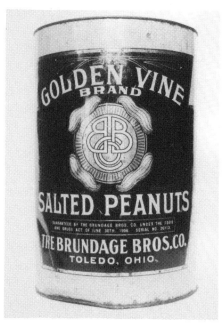

Golden Vine, round, lithograph, 11¼ × 7½, **$45**

Lion, round, lithograph, 11½ × 8, **$50**

Giant, pail, lithograph, 3 × 4, **$150**

Lion, round, lithograph, 9½ × 9, **$50**

Lotus Brand, round, lithograph,
9½ × 8, **$50**

Mellonut, round, lithograph,
9½ × 8, **$50**

Lotus Brand, round, lithograph,
11½ × 7½, **$60**

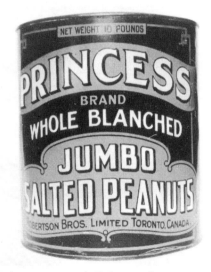

Princess, round, lithograph,
9½ × 8, **$75**

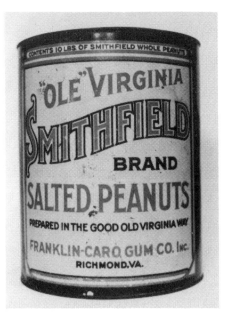

Smithfield, round, lithograph,
10 × 8½, **$50**

Sumore, round, lithograph,
10 × 8½, **$45**

Popcorn

Betty Zane, round, lithograph,
5 × 2½, **$20**

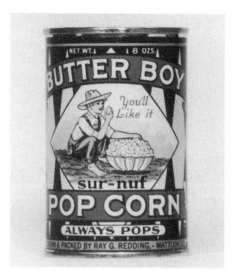

Butter Boy, round, paper label,
4 × 2½, **$35**

Danny Boy, round, lithograph,
4 × 3, **$40**

Big Buster, round, lithograph,
4½ × 2½, **$35**

Donald Duck, round, lithograph,
5 × 2½, **$45**

Gloria Jean, round, paper label,
5 × 2½, **$25**

Hopalong Cassidy's, round, lithograph, 5 × 2½, **$45**

Little Buster, round, lithograph,
4½ × 2½, **$45**

Midget, round, lithograph,
4½ × 3½, **$35**

Mor-Zip, round, paper label,
7½ × 2, **$15**

Silvertip's, round, lithograph,
4½ × 2½, **$45**

Popeye, rectangular, lithograph,
5 × 3 × 2, **$35**

Spices

Ann Page, round, cardboard,
2½ × 2¼, **$7**

A & P, round, lithograph, 3¼ × 2,
$12

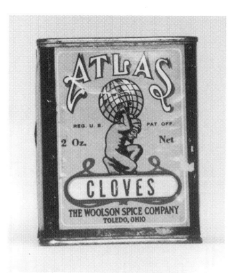

Atlas, rectangular, cardboard,
3¼ × 2¼ × 1½, **$15**

Aristo, rectangular, lithograph,
3½ × 2¼ × 1¼, **$10**

Arbuckles', rectangular, lithograph,
3¼ × 2¼ × 1¼, **$8**

Bee Brand, rectangular, lithograph,
3 × 2½ × 1¼, **$8**

Bell's, rectangular, cardboard,
3 × 2½ × 2, **$15**

Ben-Hur, rectangular, lithograph,
2 × 2½ × 1¼, **$7**

Baker's, rectangular, lithograph,
4 × 2¼ × 1½, **$10**

Ben-Hur, rectangular, lithograph,
3 × 2¼ × 1¼, **$7**

Briardale, rectangular, lithograph, 3¼ × 2½ × 1¼, **$9**

Buster Brown, rectangular, cardboard, 3¼ × 2¼ × 1¼, **$35**

Buster Brown, round, cardboard, 2½ × 2, **$35**

Buster Brown, rectangular, cardboard, 2¼ × 2 × 1½, **$35**

Canova, rectangular, lithograph, 3¼ × 2 × 1¼, **$10**

City of Lakes, rectangular, paper label, 3½ × 2¼ × 1¼, **$10**

College Town, rectangular, lithograph, 4½ × 2¼ × 1¼, **$20**

Busy Biddy, rectangular, lithograph, 3¼ × 2¼ × 1½, **$40**

Cowan's, rectangular, lithograph,
3¼ × 2 × 1¼, **$6**

Crown Colony, rectangular, lithograph, 3¼ × 2½ × 1¼, **$5**

Conquest, rectangular, lithograph,
3 × 1½ × 1, **$15**

Court House, rectangular, cardboard, 3¼ × 2 × 1¼, **$15**

Daisee, oval, lithograph,
3¼ × 2½ × 1¼, **$35**

Defiance, rectangular, cardboard,
3¼ × 2½ × 1¼, **$10**

Dining Car, rectangular, cardboard,
3¼ × 2¼ × 1¼, **$25**

Dolly Varden, rectangular, lithograph, 3¼ × 2¼ × 1¼, **$20**

Dove Brand, round, lithograph,
4 × 2, **$40**

Dove Brand, round, lithograph,
4 × 2, **$30**

Eddy's, round, cardboard,
4¼ × 1½, **$10**

Durkee's, rectangular, lithograph,
4 × 2½ × 1½, **$8**

Durkee's, rectangular, lithograph,
3¼ × 2¼ × 1¼, **$8**

Empress, rectangular, lithograph,
3¼ × 2½ × 1¼, **$15**

Fairway, rectangular, cardboard,
3¼ × 2½ × 1½, **$25**

Fame, rectangular, lithograph,
3¼ × 2½ × 1¼, **$10**

Favorite, rectangular, lithograph, 4 × 2½ × 1, **$10**

Fiesta, rectangular, lithograph, 3½ × 2¼ × 1¼, **$20**

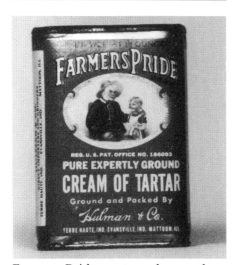

Farmers Pride, rectangular, cardboard, 3¼ × 2¼ × 1¼, **$15**

Ferndell, rectangular, lithograph, 4¼ × 1½ × 1, **$14**

Foley Bros. & Kelly, rectangular, lithograph, 9¼ × 7 × 5, **$50**

Gilt Edge, square, lithograph, 10 × 7 × 7, **$100**

Florence Nightingale, rectangular, cardboard, 2¼ × 2¼ × 1¼, **$10**

Foltz Maid, rectangular, lithograph, 3¼ × 2¼ × 1¼, **$25**

Gold Bond, rectangular, lithograph, 3¼ × 2½ × 1¼, **$10**

Gold Chord, rectangular, lithograph, 3½ × 2¼ × 1¼, **$12**

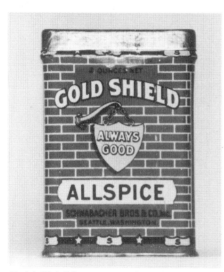

Gold Shield, rectangular, lithograph, 3¼ × 2¼ × 1¼, **$10**

Glendora, round, lithograph, 3½ × 2, **$30**

Great American, round, lithograph,
3¼ × 2, **$12**

Harvest Queen, rectangular, lithograph, 3¼ × 2½ × 1¼, **$7**

Hale's Leader, round, lithograph,
4 × 2, **$10**

Hatchet, rectangular, lithograph,
4 × 2¼ × 1½, **$10**

Hazel, rectangular, cardboard,
3¼ × 2 × 1¼, **$10**

Hillman's, rectangular, cardboard,
3½ × 2¼ × 1¼, **$10**

Hollywood, rectangular, lithograph,
3¼ × 2¼ × 1½, **$12**

Home Brand, rectangular, cardboard, 3¼ × 2¼ × 1¼, **$12**

Honest, round, paper label, 5 × 2, **$15**

Hoyt's, rectangular, lithograph, 4¼ × 2½ × 1, **$10**

Hoyt, W. M.; rectangular; lithograph; 9¼ × 7 × 5; **$100**

Ideal, rectangular, lithograph, 3¼ × 2½ × 1¼, **$8**

Ideal Brand, rectangular, lithograph, 3¼ × 2½ × 1¼, **$8**

Jack Sprat, rectangular, cardboard, 3 × 2½ × 1¼, **$12**

Jack Sprat, rectangular, cardboard, 3¼ × 2¼ × 1¼, **$18**

Jack Sprat, rectangular, cardboard, 3¼ × 2¼ × 1¼, **$25**

Kamo, rectangular, cardboard,
3¼ × 2¼ × 1¼, **$20**

Keystone, rectangular, lithograph,
3 × 2¼ × 1¼, **$7**

Keen's, odd, lithograph,
5½ × 8 × 6, **$75**

Lake View, rectangular, lithograph,
3¼ × 2¼ × 1¼, **$18**

Ko-Zee Inn, rectangular, paper
label, 3 × 2 × 1¼, **$12**

LC, rectangular, cardboard,
3¼ × 2 × 1¼, **$9**

Lanco, rectangular, cardboard,
3¼ × 2½ × 1¼, **$12**

Little Elf, rectangular, lithograph,
3¼ × 2½ × 1¼, **$18**

Lange's, round, lithograph,
5¼ × 2, **$10**

Lee, rectangular, lithograph,
3 × 2¼ × 1¼, **$8**

Maltese Cross, rectangular, lithograph, 3 × 2¼ × 1¼, **$15**

Market Basket, rectangular, cardboard, 3¼ × 2½ × 1¼, **$6**

McMurray's, rectangular, cardboard, 3¼ × 2¼ × 1½, **$9**

Mohican, rectangular, lithograph, 2½ × 2½ × 1¼, **$15**

Monarch, rectangular, cardboard, 3¼ × 2½ × 1¼, **$10**

Mother Dawson, rectangular, lithograph, 4 × 2½ × 1½, **$20**

Muscatine, rectangular, lithograph, 9¼ × 7 × 5, **$50**

Nabob, rectangular, lithograph,
3¼ × 2¼ × 1, **$8**

Natco, rectangular, cardboard,
3¼ × 2½ × 1¼, **$6**

Nectar Brand, slant front, lithograph, 10½ × 9 × 6, **$95**

Old Mansion, rectangular, lithograph, 4¼ × 2¼ × 1¼, **$15**

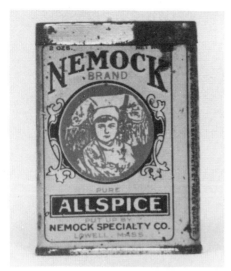

Nemock, rectangular, lithograph, 3½ × 2½ × 1¼, **$15**

Old Judge, rectangular, cardboard, 3½ × 2¼ × 1¼, **$10**

Our Family, rectangular, cardboard, 3 × 2¼ × 1¼, **$8**

Paradise Farm, rectangular, paper label, 3 × 2 × 1½, **$12**

Parke's Newport, round, lithograph, 4 × 2, **$30**

Pocono, round, cardboard, 4 × 2½, **$12**

Pocono, rectangular, lithograph, 3¼ × 2¼ × 1¼, **$15**

President, rectangular, cardboard, 3¼ × 2¼ × 1¼, **$25**

Puck, rectangular, cardboard,
3½ × 2 × 1¼, **$15**

Rawleigh's, rectangular, lithograph,
3½ × 2 × 1¼, **$7**

Princess, rectangular, lithograph,
3¼ × 2½ × 1¼, **$20**

Richelieu, rectangular, lithograph,
3½ × 1½ × 1, **$10**

Red Owl, rectangular, lithograph, 2½ × 2¼ × 1¼, **$6**

Red & White, rectangular, lithograph, 2½ × 2¼ × 1¼, **$15**

Sauer's, rectangular, lithograph, 3¼ × 2½ × 1¼, **$6**

S & F, rectangular, lithograph, 3 × 2¼ × 1¼, **$5**

Royal Boy, rectangular, cardboard, 2½ × 2 × 1½, **$35**

Snow-Ball, rectangular, lithograph, 3 × 2¼ × 1¼, **$15**

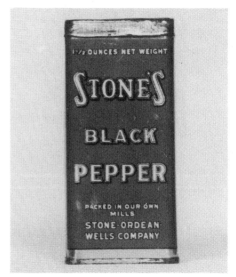

Stone's, rectangular, lithograph, 3½ × 1½ × 1¼, **$10**

Silver Buckle, rectangular, cardboard, 2¼ × 2¼ × 1¼, **$15**

Slade's, round, lithograph, 4 × 1½, **$12**

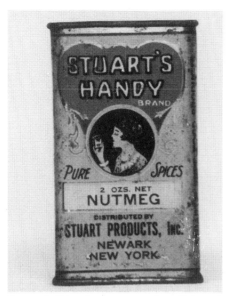

Stuart's Handy, rectangular, lithograph, 3½ × 2¼ × 1¼, **$15**

Sudan, rectangular, cardboard, 3½ × 2 × 1¼, **$10**

Sunny Brook, rectangular, cardboard, 3¼ × 2 × 1¼, **$15**

T & T, rectangular, lithograph, 3 × 2½ × 1¼, **$5**

Temple Garden, rectangular, card-board, 3½ × 1¼ × 1, **$15**

Turkey Red, rectangular, litho-graph, 3 × 2¼ × 1¼, **$25**

Time O' Day, rectangular, litho-graph, 2½ × 2 × 1, **$15**

Trumpet, round, cardboard, 5¼ × 2, **$15**

Tuxedo, rectangular, lithograph,
3¼ × 2¼ × 1, **$10**

Veteran Brand, rectangular, lithograph, 3¼ × 2¼ × 1¼, **$25**

Wapello Chief, square, lithograph,
4½ × 2½ × 2½, **$30**

White Horse, rectangular, cardboard, 4 × 2¼ × 1¼, **$20**

Wixon, rectangular, cardboard,
3 × 2¼ × 1¼, **$20**

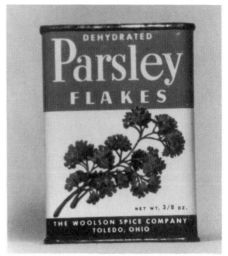

Woolson, rectangular, lithograph,
3 × 2¼ × 1¼, **$5**

Wyler's, rectangular, cardboard,
4½ × 1½ × 1¼, **$8**

Yankee Girl, round, lithograph,
4 × 2, **$25**

Syrup

Canada Sap, rectangular, paper
label, 10 × 5 × 2½, **$75**

Log Cabin, rectangular, lithograph,
3½ × 3½ × 2½, **$50**

Log Cabin, rectangular, lithograph,
3½ × 3½ × 2½, **$100**

Log Cabin, rectangular, lithograph,
3½ × 3½ × 2½, **$40**

Log Cabin, rectangular, lithograph,
3½ × 3½ × 2½, **$100**

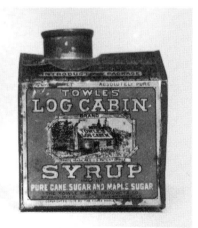

Log Cabin, rectangular, lithograph,
2½ × 2½ × 1½, **$200**

Log Cabin, rectangular, lithograph,
3½ × 3½ × 2½, **$100**

Log Cabin, rectangular, lithograph,
3½ × 3½ × 2½, **$100**

Log Cabin, rectangular, lithograph,
3½ × 3½ × 2½, **$100**

Log Cabin, rectangular, lithograph,
3½ × 3½ × 2½, **$100**

Log Cabin, rectangular, lithograph,
4½ × 5 × 3, **$150**

Log Cabin, rectangular, lithograph,
4½ × 5 × 3, **$100**

Log Cabin, round, lithograph,
3 × 4, **$100**

Log Cabin bank, rectangular, lithograph, 2½ × 3 × 2, **$200**

Long's, odd, lithograph, 4 × 3½ × 2, **$150**

Lumber Jack, square, lithograph, 9¼ × 4¼ × 3¼, **$25**

Skookum, rectangular, lithograph, 11 × 6 × 4, **$35**

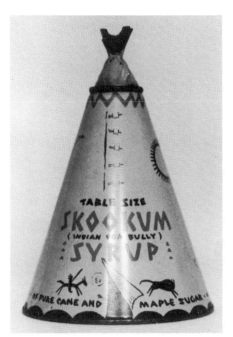

Skookum wigwam, odd, lithograph,
6 × 4, **$250**

Tea

Banquet, square, lithograph,
3 × 1½ × 1½, **$20**

Blue Ribbon, rectangular, lithograph, 9 × 7½ × 5, **$75**

CB Orient, slant front, lithograph, 7 × 5 × 5, **$75**

Choice Family, pail, lithograph, 4 × 4¼, **$40**

Canawella, square, lithograph, 8¼ × 6½ × 6½, **$50**

City Tea & Coffee, rectangular, lithograph, 9 × 7½ × 5, **$60**

Dining Car, square, cardboard, 3½ × 3 × 3, **$30**

Foltz Maid, square, lithograph, 4 × 2½ × 2½, **$45**

Grandmother's, square, lithograph, 4 × 3 × 3, **$10**

Grand Union, square, lithograph,
7¼ × 5¼ × 5¼, **$100**

Kavanaugh's, square, cardboard,
6 × 4½ × 4½, **$25**

Great Atlantic & Pacific, square,
lithograph, 10 × 7 × 7, **$200**

Jack Sprat, square, lithograph,
5 × 2½ × 2½, **$60**

Lipton, square, lithograph,
6 × 4 × 4, **$30**

Liptons, square, paper label,
6 × 4 × 4, **$25**

May Blossom, rectangular, lithograph, 7 × 7 × 4½, **$25**

Lipton's, round, paper label,
4½ × 5, **$25**

Maxwell House, square, lithograph,
4 × 2½ × 2½, **$35**

Mayfair, square, lithograph,
4 × 2½ × 2½, **$15**

Millar's, square, cardboard,
4 × 3½ × 3½, **$15**

McCormick, rectangular, lithograph, 5 × 4 × 2, **$15**

Monarch, square, lithograph,
6 × 3½ × 3½, **$35**

Monarch, square, lithograph,
6 × 3½ × 3½, **$25**

National, square, lithograph,
4 × 2½ × 2½, **$20**

Nash's, square, lithograph,
7½ × 6 × 6, **$45**

Prairie, rectangular, lithograph,
9 × 7½ × 5, **$60**

Ridgways, square, lithograph,
6 × 4 × 4, **$35**

O-Jib-Wa, round, paper label,
4½ × 3, **$25**

Oriental, square, lithograph,
7½ × 5½ × 5½, **$75**

Sahib, square, lithograph,
4 × 3½ × 3½, **$20**

Tetley's, rectangular, lithograph,
4½ × 3½ × 2, **$15**

Twilight, square, lithograph,
3½ × 2½ × 2½, **$40**

Yale, square, cardboard,
3½ × 3 × 3, **$25**

Vantine's, square, lithograph,
4½ × 2½ × 2½, **$25**

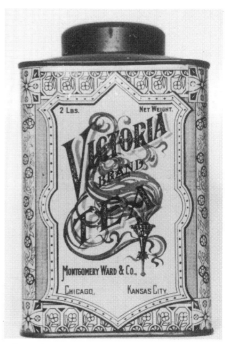

Victoria, square, lithograph,
7½ × 5½ × 5½, **$125**

White House, square, cardboard,
3½ × 3 × 3, **$80**

White Villa, square, lithograph,
4½ × 2½ × 2½, **$25**

Miscellaneous

Arm & Hammer baking soda, rectangular, lithograph, 4 × 3 × 1½, **$35**

American barley, round, cardboard, 6 × 2½, **$20**

Cherokee green beans, round, paper label, 4½ × 3½, **$15**

Columbia ginger, rectangular, lithograph, 1½ × 5 × 3½, **$16**

Cracker Jack, round, lithograph, 6¼ × 5¼, **$45**

First American peas, round, paper label, 4½ × 3½, **$15**

Ferndell ginger, rectangular, lithograph, 1½ × 3 × 2, **$12**

Heinz fig pudding, round, lithograph, 2½ × 4½, **$15**

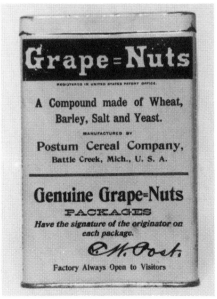

Grape-Nuts, rectangular, lithograph, 6 × 3 × 2, **$50**

Imperial ginger, rectangular, lithograph, 1½ × 5 × 3½, **$12**

Hammond lard, pail, lithograph, 5 × 5, **$35**

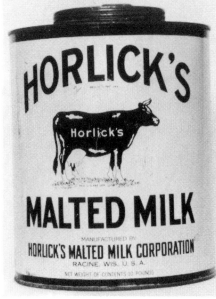

Horlick's malted milk, round, lithograph, 9 × 8, **$40**

Lakeland biscuits, square, lithograph, 5 × 9 × 9, **$35**

Little Chief shortening, pail, lithograph, 9 × 9, **$35**

Maryland Chief vegetables, round, paper label, 4½ × 3½, **$15**

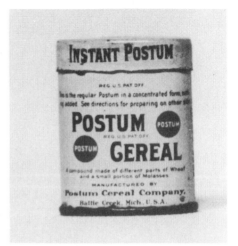

Pikes Peak Brand lard, pail, lithograph, 8 × 7½, **$25**

Postum Cereal (sample), rectangular, lithograph, 1½ × 1 × 1½, **$35**

Teenie Weenie corn, round, paper label, 4½ × 3½, **$25**

Sewansecott oysters, round, lithograph, 4 × 3¼, **$10**

Tippecanoe, round, paper label,
4½ × 3½, **$20**

Sunshine crackers, rectangular,
lithograph, 7 × 9 × 7, **$45**

About the Author

Al Bergevin and his wife, Marlene, have been in the antiques business for over 16 years. Mr. Bergevin has been buying, selling, and collecting advertising items over that period of time. This is his second book; his first is about tobacco tins. He and his wife attend shows all over the country; they reside in Minnesota.